# Hello Grandma!

Story by Leonie Bennett
Pictures by Jan McCafferty

We got in a taxi.

We got in a train.

We went on a bus.

# We went on a plane.

We had dinner on the plane.
We had tea on the plane.

We went to sleep on the plane, too.

We got off the plane and we saw Grandma!

Hello Grandma!

We went in a taxi.
We went on a bus.
We went on a train.
We went on a plane.